To Ara, Willa, and all my adult Swifties—KM

To Ricky and Bolu, love you to
the moon and to Saturn—YM

PENGUIN WORKSHOP
An imprint of Penguin Random House LLC
1745 Broadway, New York, New York 10019

First published in the United States of America by Penguin Workshop,
an imprint of Penguin Random House LLC, 2025

Visit us online at penguinrandomhouse.com.

Library of Congress Cataloging-in-Publication Data is available.

Manufactured in China

ISBN 9798217052059
10 9 8 7 6 5 4 3 2 1
HH

The text is set in Adobe Garamond Pro.
The art was created using a gouache brush in Adobe Photoshop.

Design by Taylor Abatiell

TAYLOR SWIFT

A Who Was? ILLUSTRATED BIOGRAPHY

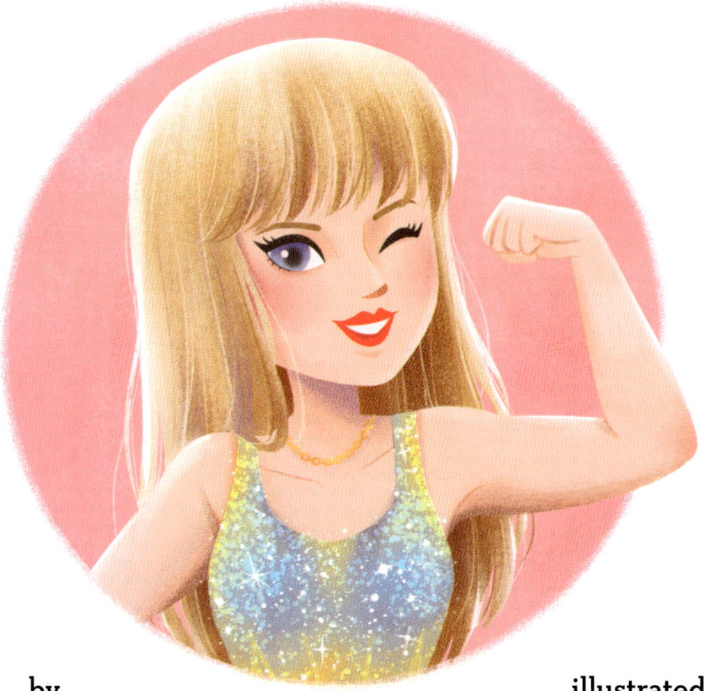

by
Kirsten Mayer

illustrated by
Yenna Mariana

PENGUIN WORKSHOP

The Bluebird Cafe does not look like a famous restaurant from the outside, but music fans know about this special place in Nashville, Tennessee. Many legendary musicians have been on its humble stage.

In the fall of 2004, a blond fourteen-year-old girl with a guitar sang a few songs for the crowd. She was good. So good that her brief appearance would lead to a deal with a record company.

Who was this young musician?

On December 13, 1989, the Swift family welcomed a new baby girl. They named her Taylor Alison Swift. As she grew up, her parents and younger brother could see that she loved performing and making music. Her grandmother Marjorie would sing and play piano with her.

Her mom was always her best friend, and her
dad wasn't afraid to dream big for his little girl.
The family moved closer to Nashville so that Taylor
could pursue a career in music.

At age twelve, she learned to play a twelve-string
guitar even though someone said her hands were
too small. "Anytime someone tells me that I can't do
something, I want to do it more," said Taylor.

Taylor started writing songs to help deal with school and friends. "I would say to myself, 'It's okay, you can write a song about this later,'" she explained.

At fourteen, she was hired to write music and lyrics professionally. Taylor always brought a lot of ideas to her adult cowriters. "I wanted them to look at me as a person they were writing with, not a little kid," she said.

The teenager made recordings of herself performing and sent them out to professionals in the country music world. Her efforts worked, and someone wanted to release her album! It was exciting, but the company wanted to wait a few years—and Taylor did not. That was how she ended up at the Bluebird Cafe getting herself a better deal.

Taylor Swift, her first album, was released in 2006 when Taylor was sixteen. At the time, no one thought that young people listened to country music. However, Taylor knew *she* loved it, and since her songs were about her own life, she knew other young people would like them, too.

Taylor trusted herself, but she also put in a lot of hard work to share her music. She traveled all over the United States, performing wherever and whenever she could.

All that effort won Taylor her first Country Music Award and sold enough copies of her album that the record company wanted more music. Over the next five years, Taylor quickly released the albums *Fearless*, *Speak Now*, and *Red*. She loved trying new things, even when it made her nervous. She had small acting roles in television and film, and wrote songs for movies, television, and other artists.

As her success grew, some people suggested Taylor was not really writing her own music. No one could believe that someone her age had achieved so much! She wrote all the songs on her *Speak Now* album by herself, without any cowriters, to prove that she could. "Songwriting has always been the number one thing. . . . If I didn't write, I wouldn't sing," she said.

41
CMA | HORIZON AWARDS
TAYLOR SWIFT

With her next album, *1989*, Taylor firmly moved into the genre of pop music as she experimented with different sounds. "I want to make music that reflects all of my influences." She loved all kinds of music, not just country.

By this time, she had won lots of awards and sold millions of albums. Everyone wanted to know everything about the star, and online rumors spread about her—both good and bad. So Taylor stayed out of the spotlight for a year and erased her social media. Then she started over with *Reputation*, an album about dealing with fame. It was a huge success.

Taylor was still true to herself,
still a storyteller, still writing her own songs
and saying what she wanted to say.

Taylor pushed herself to learn new ways to write and make music, but the songs always told a story, just like the country songs she grew up loving. "I love writing songs because I love preserving memories, like putting a picture frame around a feeling."

Taylor admitted that she groups her songs together in her mind. "They are affectionately titled Quill Lyrics, Fountain Pen Lyrics, and Glitter Gel Pen Lyrics," she said. Quill songs, like the old-fashioned writing pens made from feathers, are poetic and filled with fantasy. The Fountain Pen songs are more vivid and detailed, full of raw feeling. Her most danceable tunes would qualify as Gel Pen songs, with carefree words and lively beats.

Taylor released three more albums: *Lover*, *Folklore*, and *Evermore*. Despite spending months on the road touring, and writing songs every week, she thought a lot about her fans. Taylor valued what her songs meant to other people. "I want these songs to go out into the world and become whatever my fans want them to be."

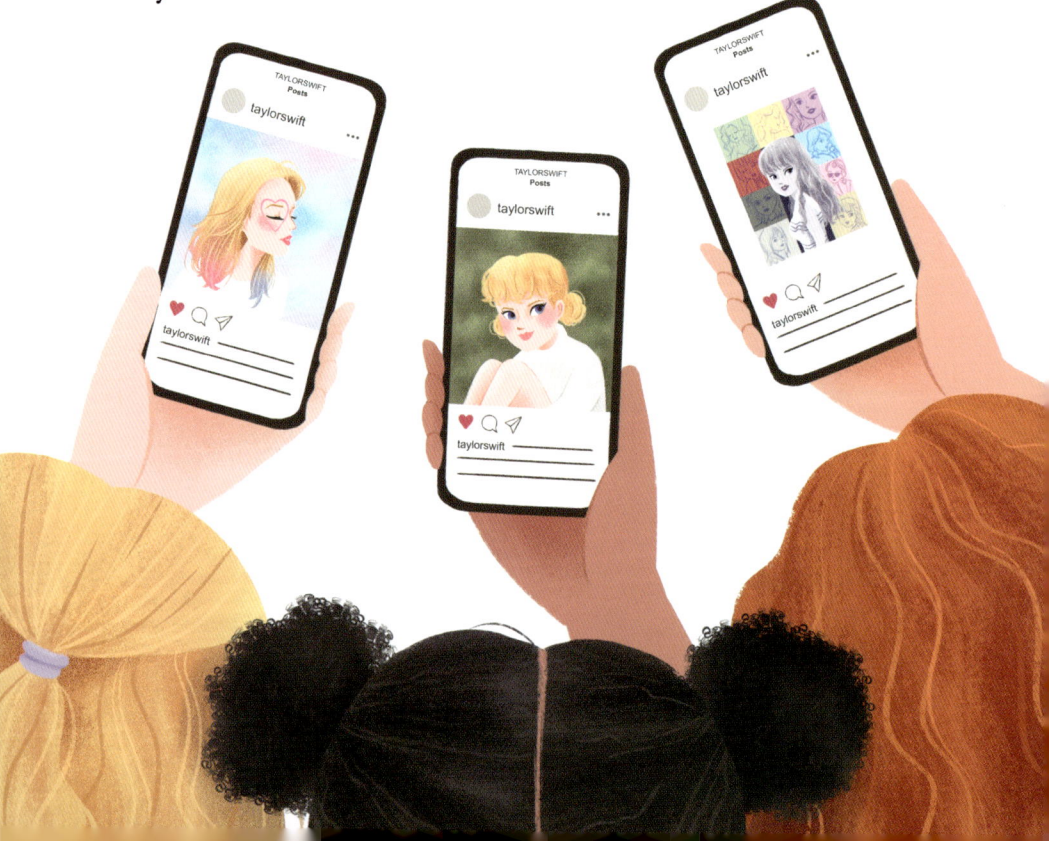

She began to put little hints out before album and song releases, and then make surprise announcements at award shows. Her fans, called Swifties, learned to start looking for these secret messages in her social media posts and album notes. Taylor used colors, numbers, and Morse code, and even sent messages with her clothing.

On her tours, she worked hard to entertain the crowds and make the experience special. During the Eras Tour in 2023–2024, each show was three hours or longer and covered songs from all her albums. The tour featured dozens of costumes, an amazing band, talented dancers, and incredible backup singers onstage with her.

With over 150 tour stops and a movie theater release, the Eras Tour became the most successful concert tour of all time. It even boosted business for all the towns she visited and added billions of dollars to the United States economy!

Crack the Code

Become a Swiftie by learning to recognize the secret messages Taylor Swift puts in her clothing, videos, and social media posts. Start with these numbers and colors that represent her albums.

1. *Taylor Swift* — Green
2. *Fearless* — Yellow
3. *Speak Now* — Purple
4. *Red* — Red
5. *1989* — Light Blue
6. *Reputation* — Black
7. *Lover* — Pink
8. *Folklore* — Gray
9. *Evermore* — Brown
10. *Fearless (Taylor's Version)* — Yellow
11. *Red (Taylor's Version)* — Red
12. *Midnights* — Dark Blue
13. *Speak Now (Taylor's Version)* — Purple

Bonus Secret

There is a lyric in the song "You're on Your Own, Kid" about friendship bracelets that has inspired fans to make bracelets with Taylor's album titles, lyrics, and other catchphrases to trade with each other at her concerts. "So, make the friendship bracelets, take the moment and taste it."

Taylor knew she owed her success to her fans. She loved to surprise them. She has invited fans to listen to albums early, dropped in on weddings and parties, and even stopped by and rung the doorbell at some fans' homes!

She also donated money to help people who
need it. Large donations went to charitable
organizations and disaster relief, but Taylor has
also helped individual fans pay their bills or pay off
student loans, like a fairy godmother!

When she wasn't onstage, she loved to spend time with her family, hang out with her friends, and bake goodies.

Taylor loved the fall and winter seasons when she could be cozy in her sweaters and bake lots of treats. She loved her three cats even more! The star brought them on tour with her around the country, and they even appeared on her holiday card!

With her fame came more power to control her own career, and Taylor showed her skill as a businesswoman. She fought for the rights to her early recordings, but she was unable to get them from her first record company. So she began recording her early albums all over again and releasing her own versions.

Taylor Swift was a star on her own terms.

Swift also spoke out on behalf of all artists who deserved to be paid fairly by streaming services. She said that "music is art and art is important and rare." She wanted the music industry to benefit the musicians, not just big companies. "For any little kid who's taking piano lessons right now," she said, "I want them to have an industry to go into."

Lucky Numbers

Taylor is humble about her achievements, but it's hard to hide her success. Here are a few of her record-breaking numbers.*

- 8 Academy of Country Music Award wins
- 11 original albums featuring 274 songs
- 12 songs at #1 on the Hot 100 *Billboard* chart
- 14 Grammy Award wins, including a record 4 Grammy Awards for Best Album
- 29 #1 songs on *Billboard*'s US Digital Song Sales chart, more than any other artist
- 40 American Music Award wins, more than any other artist
- 49 Billboard Music Award wins
- 1,603 total award nominations, and 682 wins
- 232 songs on the Hot 100 *Billboard* chart
- 1,000,000,000 Spotify streams for *The Tortured Poets Department* in its first week, a record

*As of March 2025.

The young girl who grew from playing piano with her grandmother into one of the world's biggest superstars is also just a normal person, and she fights to always remain true to herself. Taylor Swift is a songwriter, a singer, a guitarist, a pianist, a director, and more. "I am imaginative, I am smart, and I'm hardworking," she said.

Taylor Swift has proven over and over again that a young woman should never be underestimated.

Bibliography

*Books for young readers

*Anderson, Kirsten. *Who Is Taylor Swift?* New York: Penguin Workshop, 2024.

Hunt, Helena, editor. *Taylor Swift: In Her Own Words*. Chicago: Agate Publishing, Inc., 2019.

*Loggia, Wendy. *Taylor Swift: A Little Golden Book Biography*. New York: Golden Books, 2023.

McHugh, Carolyn. *Taylor Swift Superstar: The Illustrated Biography Album by Album*. Chicago: Sona Books, 2024.

*Sánchez Vergara, Maria Isabel. *Little People, BIG DREAMS: Taylor Swift*. London, UK: Frances Lincoln Children's Books, 2024.

Wilson, Lana, director. *Miss Americana*. Tremolo Productions, 2020.

Wrench, Sam, director. *Taylor Swift: The Eras Tour*. Taylor Swift Productions, 2023.

Website

www.taylorswift.com

Taylor's Discography

Taylor Swift
October 24, 2006

Fearless
November 11, 2008
*Taylor's Version
released 2021*

Speak Now
October 25, 2010
*Taylor's Version
released 2023*

Red
October 22, 2012
*Taylor's Version
released 2021*

1989
October 27, 2014
*Taylor's Version
released 2023*

Reputation
November 10, 2017

Lover
August 23, 2019

Folklore
July 24, 2020

Evermore
December 11, 2020

Midnights
October 21, 2022

The Tortured Poets Department
April 19, 2024

TIMELINE

1989 — Taylor Alison Swift is born December 13 in West Reading, Pennsylvania

2004 — Moves with her family to a town near Nashville, Tennessee, called Hendersonville

— Performs at the Bluebird Cafe for the first time

2006 — Releases her first single, titled "Tim McGraw"

2009 — Appears in a small role on the television show *CSI: Crime Scene Investigation*

Becomes the youngest person ever to win Album of the Year at the Grammy Awards — **2010**

Brings home a Scottish fold cat and names her Meredith Grey — **2011**

Brings home a second Scottish fold cat and names her Olivia Benson — **2014**

Returns to the Bluebird Cafe for a surprise performance — **2018**

Takes home the cat featured in her music video for "ME!" and names him Benjamin Button — **2019**

Rerecordings of her first albums, called "Taylor's Version," begin to release — **2021**

Begins her Eras Tour — **2023**